CAREER
ANCHORS

THIRD EDITION

Edgar H. Schein

Pfeiffer
A Wiley Imprint
www.pfeiffer.com

Published by Pfeiffer
An Imprint of Wiley
989 Market Street, San Francisco, CA 94103-1741
www.pfeiffer.com

For additional copies/bulk purchases of this book in the U.S. please contact 800-274-4434.

Pfeiffer books and products are available through most bookstores. To contact Pfeiffer directly call our Customer Care Department within the U.S. at 800-274-4434, outside the U.S. at 317-572-3985, fax 317-572-4002, or visit www.pfeiffer.com.

Pfeiffer also publishes its books in a variety of electronic formats. Some content that appears in print may not be available in electronic books.

ISBN-10: 0-7879-8428-0
ISBN-13: 978-0-7879-8428-1

Acquiring Editor: Lisa Shannon
Director of Development: Kathleen Dolan Davies
Developmental Editor: Susan Rachmeler
Production Editor: Dawn Kilgore
Editor: Rebecca Taff
Manufacturing Supervisor: Becky Carreño

Printed in the United States of America
Printing 10 9 8 7 6 5 4 3 2 1

Contents

Introduction

THE PURPOSE OF THIS SELF-ASSESSMENT is to help you to manage your career choices. A self-analysis of your career up to this point is essential if you are to make good choices as you look ahead. Why is this important? In many occupations and organizations, careers are either over-managed or not managed at all. You either have to conform to choices that others are making for you or you get the message that you had better manage your own career or you may not get anywhere. Career counselors, coaches, personnel managers, and supervisors may be ready to tell you what your next move should be, whether or not to accept a promotion, whether or not to go into a different field, and so on. Unfortunately, even if they claim to have your interests at heart, their suggestions are inevitably geared more to the needs of the organization than to *your* needs and values.

There is overwhelming evidence that, in an increasingly complex and global world, individuals have to become more self-reliant. But you cannot be more self-reliant if you do not have a clear concept of what you are good at, what you value, and what motivates you. This self-image of competence, motives, and values is your "career anchor." This self-concept helps you make choices that are in *your* interest rather than in the interests of your employers or your occupation.

The questionnaire in this booklet is designed to help you to identify your career anchor and to think about how your motives, competencies, and values relate to your career choices. When you know your career anchor, you empower yourself to confront career choices and decisions in a manner consistent with what you truly value and how you really see yourself.

Your *career anchor* is that combination of perceived areas of competence, motives, and values that *you discover you would not give up* if you faced a career decision that might not allow you to fulfill it. It represents your real self. Without knowledge of your anchor, outside incentives might tempt you into situations or jobs that subsequently are not satisfactory because you feel that "this is not really me." The questionnaire in this booklet is intended to help you to figure out who you really are and, thereby, to avoid making bad choices. The career anchor categories also provide a simple vocabulary to enable you to talk more easily about your career goals and aspirations.

Research on career anchors has shown that most people see themselves in terms of the eight categories that will be described in the following sections of this booklet. These categories are based on extensive research conducted over the last several decades, but they should be viewed more as guidelines to help you sort out your own priorities, not as absolute career types.

Career Anchors Self-Assessment

FOR EACH OF THE FORTY ITEMS THAT FOLLOW, rate how true that statement is for you.

Rate it as 1 if it is *never* true for you

Rate it as 2 if it *seldom* true for you

Rate it as 3 if it is *often* true for you

Rate it as 4 if it is *always* true for you

Note: This is not a standardized test. The items are designed to help you think about what you want out of your career, what your areas of competence are, and what most satisfies you. You are not being scored by someone else, and your scores are not being compared to others. You are trying to figure yourself out, so try to be as honest with yourself as possible. On page 5 you will find a scoring sheet. You can transfer your self-rating for each item directly onto the scoring sheet.

Never	**Seldom**	**Often**	**Always**
1	**2**	**3**	**4**

_____ 1. I want to be so good at what I do that others will always seek my expert advice.

_____ 2. I am most fulfilled in my work when I have been able to integrate the efforts of others toward a common task.

_____ 3. I dream of having a career that will allow me the freedom to do a job in my own way and on my own schedule.

_____ 4. I am always on the lookout for ideas that would permit me to start my own enterprise.

_____ 5. Security and stability are more important to me than freedom and autonomy.

_____ 6. I would rather leave my organization than be put into a job that would compromise my ability to pursue personal and family concerns.

_____ 7. I will feel successful in my career only if I have a feeling of having made a real contribution to the welfare of society.

_____ 8. I dream of a career in which I will always have the challenge of solving ever more difficult problems.

_____ 9. I will feel successful in my career only if I can develop my skills to an ever-increasing level of competence.

_____ 10. I dream of being in charge of a whole organization.

_____ 11. I am most fulfilled in my work when I am completely free to define my own tasks, schedules, and procedures.

_____ 12. I would not stay in an organization that would give me assignments that would jeopardize my job security.

_____ 13. Building a business of my own is more important to me than being a high-level manager in someone else's organization.

_____ 14. I have felt most fulfilled in my career when I have been able to use my talents in the service of others.

Never	Seldom	Often	Always
1	**2**	**3**	**4**

_____ 15. I will feel successful in my career only if I have met and overcome increasingly difficult challenges.

_____ 16. I dream of a career that will permit me to integrate my personal, family, and work needs.

_____ 17. Becoming a senior functional or technical manager in my area of expertise is more attractive to me than becoming a general manager.

_____ 18. I will feel successful in my career only if I achieve complete autonomy and freedom to define my work.

_____ 19. I usually seek jobs in organizations that will give me a sense of stability and security.

_____ 20. I feel most fulfilled when I have been able to build something that is primarily the result of my own skill and effort.

_____ 21. I will feel successful only if I become a high-level general manager in some organization.

_____ 22. Using my talents to make the world a better place to live is what drives my career decisions.

_____ 23. I have been most fulfilled in my career when I have been able to solve seemingly unsolvable problems or won out over seemingly impossible odds.

_____ 24. I feel successful in life only if I have been able to balance my personal, family, and career requirements.

_____ 25. I dream of a career that will allow me to feel a sense of stability and security.

_____ 26. I would rather leave my organization than to accept a rotational assignment that would take me out of my area of expertise.

_____ 27. Balancing the demands of my personal and professional life is more important to me than a high-level managerial position.

_____ 28. I dream of being in a career that makes a real contribution to humanity and society.

Never	**Seldom**	**Often**	**Always**
1	2	3	4

_____ 29.   I will feel successful in my career only if I have created an enterprise of my own based on my own ideas and skills.

_____ 30.   Becoming a general manager is more attractive to me than becoming a senior functional manager in my area of expertise.

_____ 31.   The chance to do a job in my own way, free of rules and constraints, is very important to me.

_____ 32.   I prefer work opportunities that strongly challenge my problem-solving and competitive skills.

_____ 33.   I dream of starting up and building my own business.

_____ 34.   I would rather leave my organization than accept a position that would undermine my ability to be of service to others.

_____ 35.   I am most fulfilled in my work when I have been able to use my special skills and talents.

_____ 36.   I would rather leave my organization than accept a job that would take me away from the path to general management.

_____ 37.   I am most fulfilled in my work life when I feel that I have complete financial and employment security.

_____ 38.   I would rather leave my organization than accept a job that would reduce my autonomy and freedom.

_____ 39.   I have always sought out work opportunities that minimize interference with my personal and family concerns.

_____ 40.   Working on problems that are difficult to solve is more important to me than achieving a high-level managerial position.

Now please go back over all of the items and locate the five that are most clearly descriptive of how you feel. Circle those items and give each of those items an additional five points on the scoring sheet.

Scoring Instructions

1. If you have not already done so, transfer your ratings for each item to the scoring table below, being sure to put the correct number of points for each item next to that item's number.

2. Add up the numbers in each column. The higher the number, the more that column represents your career anchor and preferences *as expressed by you*. The more honest you were with your answers, the more accurate the score will be. To find out what the scores mean, go on to the next section.

TF	GM	AU	SE	EC	SV	CH	LS
1_____	2_____	3_____	5_____	4_____	7_____	8_____	6_____
9_____	10_____	11_____	12_____	13_____	14_____	15_____	16_____
17_____	21_____	18_____	19_____	20_____	22_____	23_____	24_____
26_____	30_____	31_____	25_____	29_____	28_____	32_____	27_____
35_____	36_____	38_____	37_____	33_____	34_____	40_____	39_____
Total___	Total___	Total___	Total___	Total___	Total___	Total___	Total___

Description of Career Anchor Categories

FOLLOWING IS A DESCRIPTION of the eight anchor categories that have consistently shown up in all kinds of occupations. After each description, you will find two short examples that help illustrate how the anchor functions and its impact on career decision making.

The first two anchors to be described—"technical functional competence" and "general managerial competence"—revolve around a dominant sense of what one is *competent* at.

1. TF—Technical/Functional Competence

If you scored highest in this column, your career anchor is competence in some technical or functional area. What you would not give up is the opportunity to apply your skills in that area and to continue to develop those skills to an ever-higher level. You derive your sense of identity from the exercise of your skills and are most happy when your work permits you to be challenged in those areas. You may be willing to manage others in your technical or functional area, but you are not interested in management for its own sake and would avoid general management because you would have to leave your own area of expertise. The biggest problem for people with this anchor is that they tend to be pulled into generalist managerial jobs in which they may fail and that they will hate.

TF Examples

Ted Friedman graduated from business school with an interest in manufacturing engineering and had a series of jobs with a large multinational manufacturing firm that led ultimately to a promotion to manage the entire engineering group of the French subsidiary. Ted was very successful in this job and knew that he would now be considered for a major line job such as heading the whole French subsidiary. Rather than allowing himself to be considered for the job of president of that subsidiary, he lobbied with his friends in headquarters and secured a senior staff job in the manufacturing organization from which he ultimately retired. He viewed all general management jobs as too political, too fraught with personnel issues, and not really challenging.

Tania Field entered her career as a product manager in a large food company. The job required talent in marketing, and Tania discovered that she loved it and was good at it. Because of her success, she was promoted to larger and larger products, eventually taking over a product group. Although she did not enjoy management per se, she was good at it, leading the company eventually to promote her to be president of one of the divisions. She was successful in this job for ten years and was then moved into the corporate headquarters to be a senior vice president of marketing. Although she now had only a staff of one and no line responsibilities, she said, "Finally I am getting to do what I always wanted to do, set marketing strategy. I was able to be a general manager, but never really enjoyed it. Now I am happily doing what I am good at and enjoy."

2. GM—General Managerial Competence

If you scored highest in this column, your career anchor is general managerial competence. What you would not give up is the opportunity to climb to a level high enough in an organization to enable you to integrate the efforts of others across functions and to be responsible for the output of a particular unit of the organization. You want to be responsible and accountable for total results, and you identify your own work with the success of the organization for which you work. If you are presently in a technical or functional area, you view that as a necessary learning experience and may even accept a high-level management job in that function. However, your ambition is to get to a generalist job as soon as possible. You want to be able to attribute the success of your organization or project to your own managerial capabilities based on analytical skills, interpersonal and group skills, and the emotional capacity to deal with high levels of responsibility.

GM Examples

Grace Morgan started in a large computer company as a programmer. After five years in various programming jobs, she took over a technical group and displayed some talent in managing the group. Over the next several years, she took over larger and larger groups, learning during that time a lot about finance and marketing. When a company in a similar line of business needed a new CEO, she was recruited by a headhunter for this job, took it, and has successfully run this company for the last ten years.

George Mason graduated from business school and entered a program in the telephone industry for "high potential" managers that involved annual rotations through the various business functions. George was given a chance to supervise a group and discovered that he liked working in that role and was good at it. He realized at that point that he wanted to climb the managerial ladder and became quite impatient with the slow rotational program. He and a friend decided to buy a small company so that George could try his hand at running a company sooner than would have been possible in the telephone company. He successfully ran this company for twenty years and retired from that job.

The next four anchor types—"autonomy/independence," "security/stability," "entrepreneurial creativity," and "service/dedication to a cause"—revolve around a dominant *motive or need*.

3. AU—Autonomy/Independence

If you scored highest in this column, your career anchor is autonomy/independence. What you would not give up is the opportunity to define your own work in your own way. You have discovered that above all else you need to feel free and on your own in what you do in your career. Some traditional organizational jobs allow a great deal of this kind of freedom, but often people with this anchor opt for self-employment or for jobs that are highly autonomous. They can be freelance consultants, professors, independent small businessmen, field salespersons, and so forth. If you are stuck in an organization, you want to remain in jobs that allow you flexibility regarding when and how to work. You sometimes will turn down opportunities for promotion or advancement in order to retain autonomy.

AU Examples

Arthur Unger started his career in the personnel department of a large corporation and quickly discovered that he neither liked nor respected many of the rules and rituals of that organization. He tried developing a more autonomous research role, but he found that life in a large organization was just too intrusive. He left the organization and attempted freelance consulting. When he married and had children, he realized that he could not support his family from consulting work and could not raise a family with such a heavy travel schedule, so he and his wife bought and successfully ran a small store.

Alice Updike started her career as a management consultant and was so successful that she had to hire several others to handle all of the business. As her company grew, she realized that she did not like managing the organization. What she liked was the consulting and the freedom that it provided. So she sold her company and went back to being a freelance consultant.

4. SE—Security/Stability

If you scored highest in this column, your career anchor is security/stability. What you would not give up is employment security or tenure in a job or organization. Your main concern is to achieve a sense of having stabilized your career so that you can relax. The anchor can show up in concern for financial security (such as pension and retirement plans) or employment security or geographic stability in the sense of being in an area where you feel you can always find a job. Such stability may involve trading your loyalty and willingness to do whatever the employer wants from you for some promise of job tenure. You are less concerned with the content of your work and the rank you achieve in the organization, although you may achieve a high level if your talents permit. As with autonomy, everyone has certain needs for security and stability, especially at times when financial burdens may be heavy or when one is facing retirement. However, people anchored in this way are *always* concerned with these issues and build their entire self-image around the management of security and stability. They feel that they can relax only when they have achieved a position of career success and stability that allows them the feeling of having "made it."

SE Examples

Sally Evans grew up in a family that could barely afford to send her to college, and she chose engineering as her major because it would guarantee a sufficient education in four years to be able to go directly into a job without graduate training. After graduation, she went to work for a large electronics firm and developed a set of skills that she knew would be needed indefinitely. She was content with the good benefits and generous retirement plans, often accepting assignments that were not particularly challenging but that signaled her loyalty and reliability.

Stan Ebert grew up in a small town in which his father had a small business. After college, Stan worked in two or three companies that moved him around in various functions. He felt he learned a lot, but he really wanted to settle down and raise a family. He returned to his hometown and decided to enter the family business because it would provide a secure career and geographic stability.

5. EC—Entrepreneurial Creativity

If your score is highest in this column, your career anchor is entrepreneurial creativity. What you would not give up is the opportunity to create an organization or enterprise of your own, built on your own abilities and your own willingness to take risks and to overcome obstacles. You want to prove to the world that you can *create* an enterprise that is the result of your own effort. You may be working for others in an organization while you are learning and assessing future opportunities, but you will go out on your own as soon as you feel you can manage it. You want your enterprise to be financially successful as proof of your abilities. You measure yourself by the size of the enterprise and its success. This need is so strong that you will tolerate many failures throughout your career in the search for that ultimate success.

EC Examples

Ed Corbin started his career in engineering, but he was always on the lookout for opportunities to start something of his own. He developed some skills in the area of finance and discovered that certain financial procedures that were very successful in one industry were totally lacking in another industry. He moved to Denver, where he saw the opportunity to create a consulting company that would sell this new financial tool and built up a multi-million-dollar business. He also wanted to open some retail fish stores that sold ocean fish in this "mountain area," but this business failed for lack of a market. He sold the financial business and invested in some mining interests and eventually retired from being an entrepreneur to become a dean of a new business school in the area, yet another type of entrepreneurial venture.

Ellen Cohn started out as a part-time real estate salesperson while raising her children. During this time, she also started several "wives financial clubs," focusing on successful investing, and built a small retail jewelry business. After her children were older, she established her own real estate office. Over the next several years, she built a chain of real estate offices in her community and ended up running a fairly sizable real estate empire.

6. SV—Service/Dedication to a Cause

If you scored highest in this column, your career anchor is service/dedication to a cause. What you would not give up is the opportunity to pursue work that achieves something of value, such as making the world a better place to live, solving environmental problems, improving harmony among people, helping others, improving people's safety, curing diseases through new products, and so on. You would pursue such opportunities even if it meant changing organizations, and you would not accept transfers or promotions that would take you out of work that fulfills those values.

SV Examples

Stella Vargas was committed early in her life to improving life in organizations because she did not like what many bureaucratic policies had done to the morale of her father. After college, she sought a position in the personnel department of a large corporation that had the reputation of "caring for its people." What she really wanted was an influential position in organization development (OD), where she could influence corporate human relations policies. She knew that the career system in the company would move her through other personnel functions first and strongly resisted efforts to move her into those other functions. She convinced her bosses to move her into organization development and successfully implemented some new personnel policies based on her humanistic values. As her influence grew, other organizations noticed her work, which led eventually to her being recruited to be head of OD for a Fortune 100 company.

Stanley Van Ness majored in biology and forestry during his college and graduate school years. He became a professor and was able to work on his concerns about the environment and how corporate policies were endangering it. A major aluminum company in Australia was under several environmental restrictions on how it mined bauxite and needed to show the government that it was environmentally responsible. The company recruited Stanley and asked him to develop and implement mining policies that were environmentally sound. Stanley went to Australia and spent ten productive years implementing his ideas and only returned to academia when a new corporate administration wanted to reward him by giving him a general management job that was not in the environmental area.

The next anchor—"pure challenge"—reflects neither values nor motives, but a mixture of personality characteristics and problem-solving style.

7. CH—Pure Challenge

If you scored highest in this column, your career anchor is "pure challenge," in the sense that what you would not give up is the opportunity to work on solutions to seemingly unsolvable problems, to winning out over tough opponents, or to overcoming difficult obstacles. For you, the only meaningful reason for pursuing a job or career is that it permits you to win out over the seemingly impossible. Some people find such pure challenge in intellectual kinds of work, such as the engineer who is only interested in impossibly difficult designs; some find the challenge in complex multifaceted situations, such as the strategy consultant who is only interested in clients who are about to go bankrupt and have exhausted all other resources; some find it in interpersonal competition, such as the professional athlete or the salesperson who defines every sale as either a win or a loss. Novelty, variety, and difficulty become ends in themselves, and if something is easy it becomes immediately boring.

CH Examples

Paul Chatworth joined the U.S. Navy because he wanted adventure. He was able to join the aviation wing and became a pilot flying off aircraft carriers. He spent all of his discretionary time honing his flying skills so that if at some future time he had to confront an enemy in single aircraft-to-aircraft combat, he would prove to be the superior pilot. He kept himself fit and ready at all times, waiting for the opportunity to prove his own superiority. In sports and in games, he was extremely competitive and could never stand to lose. When his flying days were over, he reluctantly took a desk job but continued to be a fierce competitor in all of his non-job-related activities.

Pamela Chernow graduated from business school with a major in finance and took a job on Wall Street as a bond salesperson. She enjoyed the intrinsic intellectual and interpersonal challenge that this job provided. When offered an opportunity to be promoted into managing a group, she refused because she wanted the stimulus of one-to-one competition with others and the challenge of solving problems under conditions of uncertainty and incomplete information. She found the sales relationship intrinsically exciting and defined every situation as a "combat" in which either she or "the other" would "win." She was able to remain in this kind of competitive environment throughout her career.

The last anchor—"lifestyle"—is, in a certain sense, not specifically related to a career as such but to *the integration of career and family issues*. This anchor has become more prevalent as more dual-career families are finding that they must meet the demands of two different, equally valued careers.

8. LS—Lifestyle

If you scored highest in this column, your career anchor is lifestyle. What you would not give up is a situation that permits you to balance and integrate your personal needs, your family needs, and the requirements of your career. You want to make all of the major sectors of your life work together toward an integrated whole, and you therefore need to develop a career situation that provides enough flexibility to achieve such integration. You may have to sacrifice some aspects of the career—for example, a geographical move that would be a promotion but would require your spouse to give up his or her career aspirations or would require your children to leave a good school. You define success in terms broader than just career success. You feel that your identity is more tied up with how you live your total life, where you settle, how you deal with your family situation, and how you develop yourself than with any particular job or organization. People with this anchor sometimes organize their own careers around the careers of spouses, in terms of the geographic area in which they want to live, or in terms of issues such as where they want their children to grow up or go to school. Geographic issues often play a key role in that people with this anchor seek areas where both career and family needs can be optimally met. The person in this dilemma may have another anchor in one of the above categories but chooses to subordinate the expression of that anchor to the more general lifestyle issues.

LS Examples

Ludwig Schmidt was a high-potential middle manager working for a large oil company in its New York headquarters. He was on a general management track in the U.S. organization, although he was a German with a German wife. When his son was eight years old, Ludwig was offered a major promotion in the U.S. company that would require remaining in New York for the next five years. Ludwig turned down the promotion and opted instead for a lesser job in the German subsidiary because he and his wife decided that they wanted to bring up their son in the German culture and considered the next five years to be crucial in forming his identity.

Lisa Sargent, in mid-career on a general manager track, had to choose between a very large promotion in the headquarters of a company located in a rural area and a much less prestigious job in a corporation in a large urban area. Her husband was in a technical field, and his chances of finding a job in the urban area were much better, so Lisa chose the less prestigious job in order to maximize both of their chances to have satisfactory careers.

After reviewing all of the anchors, you may find yourself asking one or two questions that almost always come up.

What If I Don't Have a Clear "Highest" Score in Any Column?

There are two possible reasons for a very flat profile or ties in several columns:

1. You have not yet had to face a choice and hence do not yet know what your real anchor is. You may feel that you have two or more anchors because you are in a job that permits the expression of more than one. Try to imagine future career options that would force you to choose and see which way you would lean. For example, many people think that they can be both technical/functional and general managerial. Ask yourself whether you would rather be the executive vice president of the whole company or the senior vice president of the technical area. Most people find that they can quickly choose which is really their anchor, if forced to make a choice.

2. You have not faced enough varied occupational experience to know what your real preferences, talents, and values are. If that is the situation, try out different things on a temporary basis and see which ones work best for you. The anchor evolves with life experience and is not something that you have always had or that suddenly appears.

What If None of the Anchors Feels Like "Me"?

The purpose of this self-assessment is to increase your insight into your own career situation. You may well have an "anchor" that is different or some complex combination of the other categories. You do not have to fit into one of these categories, but you do have to get a good sense of who you are and what you are after in your career and life. Take those items for which you scored the highest and see what kind of pattern emerges if you look at them together. Develop your own self-concept from those items. The goal is self-insight, not fitting into a standard category.

Next Steps and Choices

THIS BOOKLET IS AN INTRODUCTION to career anchors and gives you a first approximation of what your anchor is. The *Career Anchors Participant Workbook* gives you (1) more general information about the career development field; (2) a more complete description of the anchors; (3) an interview protocol to analyze your career history and determine more precisely what your anchor is; (4) instructions on how to analyze your current job in terms of a role map; and (5) instructions on how to do a job/role analysis of possible future jobs you may wish to consider if you are in a career transition. In relation to planning for a future job/role, the Workbook also provides an analysis of where the world of work is going and a Self-Assessment Questionnaire to enable you to determine how you rate yourself on some of the competencies that will be needed in future jobs.